GW01006434

Barbu.

BOSTON

THE GROWTH OF THE CITY

BOSTON
THE GROWTH OF THE CITY

CHARTWELL
BOOKS, INC.

This edition published in 2007 by

CHARTWELL BOOKS, INC.
A Division of
BOOK SALES, INC.
114 Northfield Avenue
Edison, New Jersey 08837

ISBN-13: 978-0-7858-2216-5
ISBN-10: 0-7858-2216-X

© 2007 Compendium Publishing, 43 Frith Street, London,
Soho, W1V 4SA, United Kingdom

Cataloging-in-Publication data is available from the Library
of Congress

Printed and bound in China

Design: Ian Hughes/Compendium Design

Page 2: This equestrian statue of George Washington was an 1869 addition to
Boston Public Garden, which at the time were being landscaped in a formal
English tradition.
Page 4: A replica of one of the ships boarded during the Boston Tea Party is
now maintained by the city as part of a museum dedicated to the famous
incident that sparked the American Revolution.

Contents

Introduction

The skyline of modern Boston. The historic waterfront that was once one of the world's greatest ports and lined with tenement buildings populated by immigrants, has developed into a district of upscale apartment buildings, offices, cafes, and restaurants.

Introduction

On the United States' northeastern seaboard, at the mouth of the Charles River, is one of the nation's most historic cities, and one of its loveliest. Built around a natural harbor and boasting fine architecture in its old neighborhoods, as well as a lively atmosphere and dynamic economy, Boston was North America's first significant metropolis. While it has been eclipsed in terms of size and influence by numerous other American cities since its eighteenth and nineteenth century heyday, Boston remains a center of learning and home to some of the nation's best art galleries and museums. Its relatively small size belies the leading role it has played in the shaping of the United States since the earliest Colonial times.

The history of human habitation around Boston stretches back over at least seven thousand years. By the time the first European explorers arrived, the Nipmuck, Wampanoags, and Massachusetts tribes of the Algonquin Indians all had villages close by the Shawmut Peninsula on which the city would rise. Although, Boston is inextricably linked with the Puritan founders who arrived in the early seventeenth century, it is widely believed that the first people from across the Atlantic to visit the area were the Viking party under Leif Ericsson, who named the country that they discovered in about 1000AD Vinland. By the middle of the fifteenth century the waters off the New England coast were known to fishing boats out of England, France, and Spain and it is likely that their crews would have landed to dry their catch and trade with the local people. The first documented voyages along the coast date to the 1497 and 1498 expeditions of John Cabot, who is also credited with the discovery of Canada. Over the century following his visit, the area would become increasingly familiar to European traders, fishermen, and explorers.

It was not until the following century, however, that the first New England colonies appeared. The earliest settlement followed soon after King James I of England gave New England to a company from Plymouth in 1607. Unfortunately, it failed due to the unexpectedly harsh winter and returned home the following year. While the new village of Jamestown further down the coast in Virginia was more successful, it was not until 1620 when the *Mayflower*—crowded with religious dissidents—weighed anchor off Cape Cod that European settlement of New England got underway. Ten years later, eleven more ships carrying the Massachusetts Bay Company of Puritans arrived at Salem to occupy lands granted them by Charles I. Under the guidance of Governor John Winthrop, the majority of the new settlers traveled to the mouth of the Charles River where they found the secluded home of Boston's first European inhabitant, the

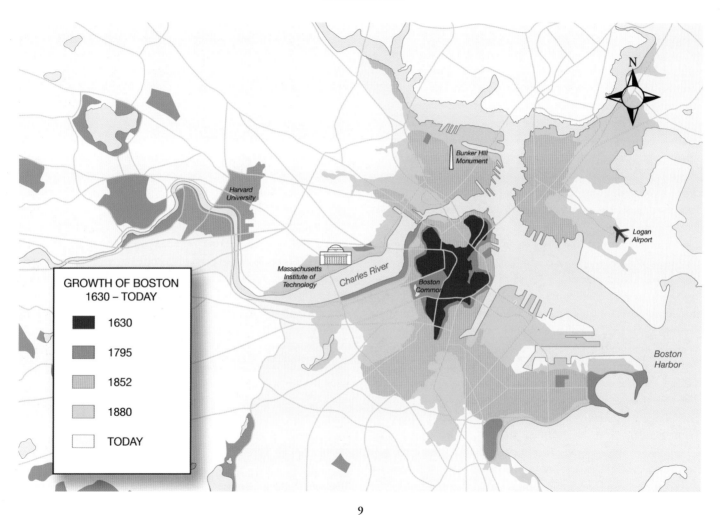

GROWTH OF BOSTON
1630 – TODAY

- 1630
- 1795
- 1852
- 1880
- TODAY

Bunker Hill Monument

Harvard University

Massachusetts Institute of Technology

Charles River

Boston Common

Logan Airport

Boston Harbor

N

Reverend William Blackstone, on Beacon Hill. At first the party established their settlement at present day Charlestown, but the lack of fresh water here meant that many of Winthrop's party soon became sick. Luckily, help was at hand. Blackstone invited the group to abandon their village and set up again close to fresh water springs on his own side of the river. His invitation was readily accepted. The settlement that had been named Trimountain (for the three hills of the peninsula) moved to the newly purchased land and was renamed in honor of the town they had left behind in England—Boston.

Boston's citizens organized their new settlement in adherence to their faith; their values of hard work, strict morality, and education meant that the fledgling town was soon stable and growing. Within a year an additional 1,500 settlers arrived from England and Boston had launched the first ship built in the city, beginning its commercial career. In 1634, the town bought forty-eight acres of land from William Blackstone as common grazing land and a military drilling ground, thus founding Boston Common. In 1635, just five years after the first settlers had arrived, Bostonians were able to open America's first school, Boston Latin School. Two years later a university was founded. The area around the college was later renamed Cambridge for the great English university city and the university itself named for John Harvard who bequeathed the institution his library. Connected to Boston by the first bridge to be built in the town in 1662, Harvard University would eventually become one of the world's most famous seats of learning.

By the end of the first decade of settlement it is estimated that a further 20,000 souls had arrived from England, though most dispersed to the surrounding countryside and the city militia could muster a 1,000 strong force on the common. Boston's first small, plain church had been replaced with a grander building on the present day site of the Roger's Building on Washington Street and America had its first post office at Fairbanks Tavern. As the center of the Massachusetts colony, smaller satellite townships were rapidly settled. Seventeenth century Boston also saw the minting of the first coins on American soil (in 1652) and in 1672 the first printing press, operated by John Foster.

The graves of Boston's first inhabitants can now be found at Copp's Hill Burying Ground, which was first used in 1659, and Boston's other early graveyards, but beyond these simple headstones, the narrow, crooked courses of a handful of streets, and the Paul Revere House, which was built in 1680, there is little to remind us of early Boston. Nevertheless, in the first seventy years of its existence the town became a busy metropolis. By the end of a century, its population had reached about 7,000 and it had transformed into a trading hub, its harbor thick with the masts of ships from foreign ports as well as those from up and down the coast. The town's shipbuilders were launching vessels by the score. Nevertheless, Bostonians still clung to their original principles. An

RIGHT: John Winthrop leads the Massachusetts Bay Company of Puritans ashore at Salem. Under his direction as a twelve-term governor of the colony, Boston was founded and the rigid religious and political policies of the early Massachusetts Bay Colony were formulated.

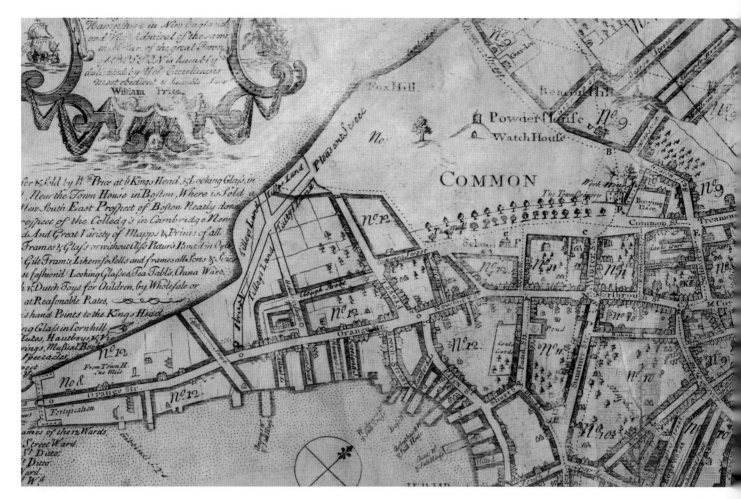

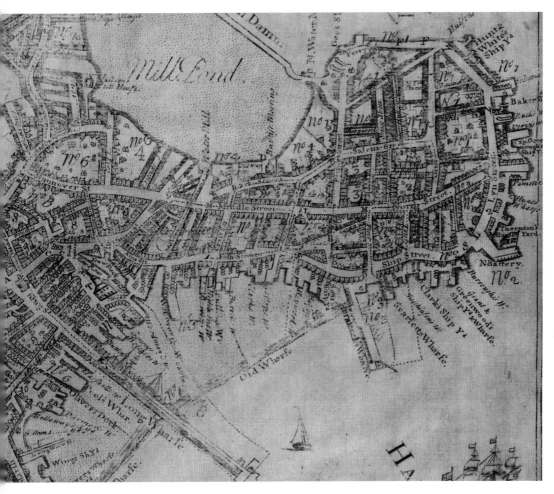

LEFT: A detail from "A new plan of ye great town of Boston in New England in America with the many additionall buildings & new streets, to the year, 1769." This fascinating old map provides a detailed overview of Boston. Described as a "flourishing town of the British Dominions in America," the map details Boston's key buildings and institutions, such as the governor's house, schools, churches, and markets, as well as dating the town's "Great Fires" and outbreaks of smallpox.

English visitor of 1799 wrote of his visit that kissing a woman in public, even as an act of simple courtesy, was punishable by the whipping of both parties. Over the preceding decades, Boston had also witnessed the expulsion and hanging of Quakers as well as the banishment of Baptists, the forced conversion of Native-Americans, and execution of many accused of witchcraft.

The beginning of the eighteenth century brought Boston the first newspaper to be published in America—the *Boston News Letter*, which began circulating in 1704—and Castle William, which was built on Castle Island in 1705. Other Boston buildings dating to the early 1800s include the Corner Book Store (1712), Old State House (1713), Boston Light (1716), Old North Church (1723), and South Meeting House (1729). As the town continued to grow in stature, however, political and military wrangling between France and Britain over the colonial territory became

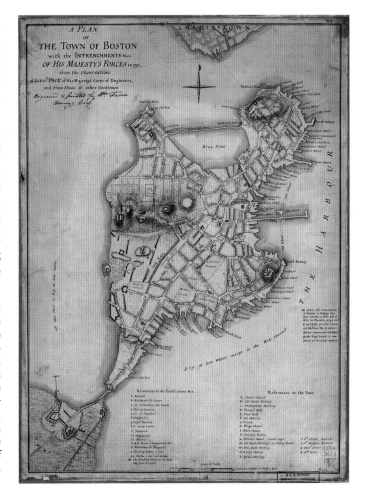

LEFT: A view of Boston dating to around 1730. Long Wharf juts out from the shore and the harbor is thick with British ships. At the time this picture was painted, Boston would have had a new addition to its streets in the South Meeting House (1729). A century after the Puritans arrived Boston's waterfront is fringed with wharves and the town is spreading over the peninsula.

RIGHT: "A Plan of the Town of Boston with the Intrenchments of His Majesty's Forces." Drawn in 1775, the key at the bottom right of the map details the extensive defenses and weapons available to the British forces occupying the city during the American Revolution, including many "24 Pounder" cannon, guard houses, blockhouses, fortifications, and even a floating battery. Nevertheless, the following year saw the army of General Washington force British troops to evacuate the town.

LEFT: Boston on November 9, 1872, with downtown in flames. Altogether 765 buildings were destroyed by the fire that started in a dry goods store. Nevertheless, the city soon recovered and from the ashes rose new industrial premises that helped the city's textile industry on to greater heights than ever before.

ABOVE: This incredibly detailed panoramic view of the city in the 1880s is not drawn to scale, nevertheless it offers an excellent sense of how Boston has grown. The Back Bay district that was once tidal marshland has been filled, steam powered mills and factories belch out smoke, trains run in and out of the city on numerous tracks and wharves and warehouses proliferate along the waterfront.

increasingly heated, culminating in the French and Indian War between the French and British, which began in 1754 and would last almost a decade. When Britain finally took control of Canada and the West from France in 1763 it looked to the colonies to help replenish coffers diminished by the conflict. Taxation imposed by the Stamp Act of 1765 and the Townshend Acts enraged colonists who were expected to pay without representation in the British Parliament. Revolutionary fervour was further inflamed by the Boston Massacre of 1770, during which five Americans died when British soldiers fired on a crowd of protestors, and reached boiling point in 1773. After a tax on tea was imposed, Bostonians dressed as Native-Americans boarded three ships of the East India Company on December 16 and turned their cargoes overboard. The Boston Tea Party heralded the American Revolution and some of the most important battles in the conflict (the battles of Lexington and Concord, Bunker Hill, and the siege of Boston) were fought in and around the city.

When the British were vanquished and peace returned to the new nation, Boston's fortunes were renewed. By 1800, the city's population had swollen to 25,000 many of whom made fortunes in trade. In fact, Boston at the turn of the nineteenth century was one of the globe's most successful and richest ports, its ships carrying tobacco, rum, fish, salt and cotton reaching as far as China. Meanwhile, early entrepreneurs opened the first textile mills, which would proliferate and place the city at the forefront of another revolution, this time industrial, later in the century. Boston was chartered as a city in 1822.

RIGHT: This postcard shows Commonwealth Avenue in Back Bay in the late nineteenth century. After the area was filled, developers were determined to make it the city's most sought-after neighborhood and followed the design of Paris, which had recently been remodeled by Baron Hausmann, in the layout of grand boulevards lined with buildings of architectural distinction.

LEFT: **A view across Boston in 1899. Note the new buildings that have grown up along Back Bay. Close to the center of the peninsula, at the eastern tip of Boston Common, is the State House. Below the common, close to the waterfront is South Union Station, which has replaced old wharves.**

With wealth came sophistication; Boston was now respected as the intellectual heart of the United States. Bostonians John Adams and his son John Quincy Adams were both elected president in 1797 and 1825 respectively while the Boston Atheneum, which housed a great library and museum, opened in 1807. Distinguished citizens included writers such as Ralph Waldo Emerson, Nathaniel Hawthorne, and Henry Wadsworth Longfellow.

The city also began to change and grow physically. The Merrimack Canal was built in 1803 linking northern Massachusetts and southern New Hampshire to Boston, while landfill began to transform the peninsula, with the city's hills being razed in order to extend the waterfront. 1804 saw Dorchester Neck and Heights annexed to become South Boston. Fine homes in the Federal style, typified by those designed by Charles Bulfinch were built, particularly on the southern slope of Beacon Hill, the neighborhood favored by the city's elite. In 1825, the Bunker Hill monument began to rise with the cornerstone laid by Lafayette himself. By 1835, the city was served by three railroads, allowing more goods than ever to flood into the city to be shipped abroad, boosting the city's prosperity still further.

As the nineteenth century progressed Boston's wealth attracted many immigrants. The population swelled dramatically in the first few decades and with the onset of the potato famine in Ireland rose more steeply still. By 1850, the city was struggling to cope with over 137,000 citizens, many of whom were poor Irish, squeezed into unsanitary and cramped tenements along the waterfront.

Twenty years later the city's population had almost doubled again, to over a quarter of a million. As the century progressed these folk, often the targets of persecution at first, would come to dominate Boston's politics and industry.

By the end of the Civil War Boston's shipping was dwindling, eclipsed by New York City down the coast, but the region's manufacturing more than compensated for the loss of income and the city continued to grow, annexing Roxbury in 1868 and Dorchester in 1870. Then, on November 9, 1872, disaster struck. Starting in a dry goods store on the corner of Summer and Kingston streets, fire swept through downtown warehouses and the financial district. Two days later when the flames were doused, sixty-five acres of the city had been destroyed and 776 buildings razed, at a cost of over sixty million dollars.

Nevertheless, with the stoic resolution that marked its founders, Boston rebuilt quickly and was soon boasting fine new buildings such as Trinity Church (1877) as well as the new parks: in 1876, Frederick Law Olmsted began landscaping the famous "Emerald Necklace," the first park system in the nation. Much of the rubble from the fire was used to create more landfill along the downtown waterfront. Other annexations (Brighton and Charlestown in 1874) and landfill projects along Back Bay and the Charles River meant that the metropolis was now bigger than ever.

As the nineteenth century drew to a close Boston remained one of the nation's most favored cities, with a robust industrial base, a successful publishing industry, museums, theaters, orchestras, widely respected universities and colleges, and even its own subway—the "T" opened in 1898, another first for Boston. At the beginning of the twentieth, Boston's citizens numbered well in excess of half a million, half of whom were Irish. As well as being an intellectual center, Boston now found itself the focus of sporting attention with the first World Series played in the city in 1903 and the first purpose built football ground, Harvard Stadium, opening the same year. Indeed, the first half of the century saw overall growth in the city, notwithstanding the deprivations of two world wars, the depression years, the Boston Molasses disaster of 1919, and turbulent city politics. Notable building projects included the Sumner Tunnel under Boston Harbor that connected North End and East Boston in 1934 and the first American housing project, built in South Boston, which welcomed its first tenants in 1936. By 1950, the population would reach an all time peak of over 800,000. Nevertheless, the winds of change were blowing. Boston saw its first mill close in 1926 and, as more and more factories shut and industry moved south where labor was cheaper, the city's fortunes slowly, but inexorably, declined.

In response to the downward spiral, Boston's politicians began an ill-conceived strategy of urban renewal that saw neighborhoods such as the Old West End and Scollay Square razed to make way

RIGHT: Looking over the peninsula in 1922, with the tower of the Custom House in the center distance. While Boston's activities as a port had declined it was still a successful commercial and industrial center at the time this photograph was taken. However, the following decades would see a slow slump in the city's economy. From 1950 onward its population also began to decline drastically.

for new municipal buildings. Others were only saved by the outrage engendered by the bulldozing of historic districts. Public pressure also meant that new plans had to be drawn up to accommodate a new highway, the Central Artery, for which parts of the financial district, Chinatown, and North End had already been demolished. From 1956, much of the new roadway would be constructed in tunnels beneath the city. Later highway and interstate developments were abandoned. In 1991, the city began the Central Artery/Tunnel project, known locally as the "Big Dig," which put the remainder of the Central Artery underground.

By the 1970s Boston's fortunes were returning again. The markets were booming and Boston took full advantage to become a financial leader, while greater numbers of students than ever were flocking to the city's prestigious universities. Many graduates stayed in the city and founded high-tech industries. More and more tourists also began to arrive to sample for themselves Boston's unique historic atmosphere. In fact, at the beginning of the new millennium, America's first city is witnessing a renaissance that indicates its future will be as bright as its past.

LEFT: A contemporary view over the common to the Financial District. In the late twentieth century Boston experienced a revival of fortunes that saw it become a center of finance, medicine, and hi-tech industry while also welcoming an increasing amount of tourists fascinated by Boston's unique place in world history.

Boston in the twenty-first century is
a city of historical winding streets
and soaring towers, mostly built on
land that did not exist when the
Puritan founders arrived.

Colonial and Revolutionary Boston: 1630–1783

Bostonians onshore cheers as demonstrators dressed in Native-American garb protest British taxes by throwing crates of tea into Boston Harbor.

Colonial and Revolutionary Boston: 1630–1783

Boston as we know it today is vastly different from the peninsula that was settled by the Massachusetts Bay Company under John Winthrop in 1630. At that time the Shawmut Peninsula covered an area of only 783 acres (compared to more than 4,000 acres today) and was connected to the mainland by a thin isthmus. Surrounded by water and marshes, the settlers on North End would have often found themselves almost cut off during high tides.

The small colony of Boston, originally numbering just 1,000 people would have been dominated by the three hills of Pemberton, Beacon, and Mount Vernon, which would later be razed to provide landfill or be lost behind a screen of skyscrapers. Their earliest buildings would have been little more than huts, built in the Native American style of wooden slates over a thin wooden frame. As the colony became more established, these

would have been superseded by the wooden Colonial-style houses that still survive in parts of New England. The single remaining example in Boston is the Paul Revere House, which was built in about 1680.

For well over a century little changed in Boston; though growth and change came, it was slow. Although, by the standards of the colonies it would have been a successful and bustling town,

Bought from Boston's original European inhabitant William Blackstone in 1634, the forty-eight acre Boston Common has since served the city as a military parade ground, pasture land, and execution site. It was also used as a camp by British forces between 1775 and 1776. The gallows were taken down in 1817 and cattle driven away in 1830 when the park was given over to recreation only. This black and white panorama dates to 1910.

and an important port, by the eve of the American Revolution, it should be remembered that the population would have only recently broken 10,000. While little is left of this period in Boston's history, traces of Colonial Boston can still be found; in the streets of the Blackstone Block, at its oldest churches, at Faneuil Hall, and at the Old Corner Bookstore. Boston had also laid the foundations of its future success as a center of learning and commerce. Harvard University opened its doors to the first nine students in 1636, while Long Wharf was complete by 1710. Industry was stirring too with the construction of a dam across North Cove, which harnessed the tide to power grist mills and sawmills. Nevertheless, the town that was at the epicentre of the American Revolution would not begin a sustained period of dramatic growth until after the nation had fought for its independence.

RIGHT AND BELOW: Although there is little to remind us of Boston's earliest days, the graves of many of its first inhabitants can be found at Copp's Hill Burial Ground (below) and the graveyard at King's Chapel (right). The 1730 gravestone of nineteen-year old Mary Moore at Copp's Hill is carved with a grim-looking winged skull, a common symbol used by early Americans to signify the soul's victory over death. The graveyard itself derives its name from local landowner William Copp from whom the land was bought in 1659 and who now rests here.

LEFT: **The Paul Revere House is the oldest surviving building in Boston and dates to 1680. At the time that Revere purchased the house (for £200) it would have had an additional storey, which has since gone, making it more consistent with the original design.**

RIGHT: As Boston's importance as a commercial hub grew and the harbor grew busier toward the end of the seventeenth century, the city looked to its port facilities. Long Wharf was completed in 1710 and could comfortably accommodate the biggest vessels of the time. In its heyday the wharf stretched about 2,000 feet into the harbor and was lined with warehouses. Today, it is still in use, making it the United States oldest operational wharf.

Harvard University

Founded just six years after the town of Boston itself, Harvard University is now well into its fourth century and is America's oldest seat of higher learning. Originally numbering nine students under a single teacher, the university is named for John Harvard who bequeathed the institution half of his estate as well as his library in 1638. In honor of the English university town, the district was also renamed Cambridge. In John Harvard's day undergraduates would have received education in the classics adapted to the Puritan beliefs with the goal of producing learned ministers for the colonies. Now it caters to over 18,000 students with a faculty of 2,000 and its curriculum has broadened to offer many hundreds of courses in the sciences as well as the arts, law, and history.

One of the world's most famous and respected universities, Harvard numbers seven presidents among its alumni as well as forty Nobel laureates. Its campus is vast and includes notable works of architecture as well as a number of museums boasting collections of fine art and archeological artifacts from around the world. At the center is Harvard Yard, which dates back to the year that the university was founded.

LEFT: This etching of the Harvard campus dates back to 1790 and shows (from left to right) Harvard, Stoughton, and Massachusetts Hall. Built in 1720, the latter is the campus's oldest surviving building. Beyond the buildings is Old Harvard Yard.

ABOVE: This photograph of the campus dates to 1910 and shows the Old Harvard Yard. The white building in the distance to the right is University Hall, which was designed by architect Charles Bulfinch in 1815. To the left is Matthews Hall.

LEFT: In Harvard Yard, before University Hall, is a statue of the university's first benefactor John Harvard, cast by Daniel Chester in 1884. Although the inscription reads "John Harvard, Founder, 1638," none of these facts is true. As no likeness of Harvard exists the statue is not of him; he was not the founder of the university; and the date should be 1636 rather than 1638.

BELOW: A 1914 game in Harvard Stadium. Built in 1903, the stadium was the first of its kind dedicated to football and has been the home to the university team ever since.

BELOW: Named for Harry Elkins Widener who perished in the *Titanic* disaster of 1912, the Widener Library contains over three million works, making it the nation's third largest library.

RIGHT: Rowers on the Charles River with Harvard Business School in the background. Inspired by the annual boat race between Oxford and Cambridge universities in Britain, Harvard has competed against Yale each year since 1852.

LEFT AND RIGHT: Seen here before its 1960s restoration, the Clough House at 21 Unity Street is a typically plain Colonial building that was the home of mason Ebenezer Clough, one of the two builders responsible for the Old North Church. Constructed in 1712, the house was neglected for years until a campaign to save it resulted in a complete overhaul. The building is now furnished in Colonial style and open to the public.

ABOVE AND RIGHT: This 1791 engraving shows Boston's State House, on Washington and State Streets. The State House was built in 1713 on the site of the colony's first town house, which was destroyed by fire in 1711. The center of government for the Massachusetts Bay Colony and later, the State of Massachusetts until the building of the new State House in 1795, the Old State House is now the city's oldest extant public building. By its east wall is a circle of stones that marks the site of the Boston Massacre of 1770.

LEFT: America's oldest continuously open restaurant is to be found on Union Street in the twisting alleys of the Blackstone Block, which trace the original streets laid out by the settlers. While Union Street itself has existed since 1636 no-one is quite sure how old the house that the restaurant now occupies is, though it is thought it was built in 1714. The Union Oyster House was opened in 1826.

RIGHT: The neighborhood of North End can trace its history back to the days of the earliest settlers, and has since welcomed immigrants of many different nationalities. The original edifice of St. Stephen's Church on Hanover Street began as a small meeting house, which was enlarged by Charles Bulfinch in 1804 and became a Catholic church in the mid-nineteenth century in order to provide the huge new Irish community in the district a place of worship. Since then this part of North End has developed an Italian flavor, thanks to subsequent immigrants.

Although this structure is a replacement for the first lighthouse that stood here, which was blown up by the British during the evacuation of 1776, the original Boston Harbor Light was the first lighthouse in America, dating to 1716.

LEFT: Seen here at around the beginning of the twentieth century, Old North Church is Boston's oldest surviving place of worship. Built in 1723, the church is famous for the part that it played in the ride of Paul Revere. On the night of April 18, 1775, Robert Newman, the sexton, signaled patriots across the river in Charlestown from here, warning them of the departure of British troops.

RIGHT: A 1900 view of Boston's Old South Meeting House, built in 1729 as a place of worship for Puritans, on the corner of Washington and Milk Streets. The church was later used for political meetings and it was here that the gathering of the Sons of Liberty was held, which led to the Boston Tea Party.

PREVIOUS PAGE, LEFT AND RIGHT:
Bequeathed to the city by Peter Faneuil in 1742, Faneuil Hall was used as a public meeting space and market and is known as the "Cradle of Liberty" for the revolutionary meetings that were held here under Samuel Adams, whose statue can now be found in front of the building. The original Georgian building has been extended twice—in 1806 and 1898—on both occasions using plans drawn up by Charles Bulfinch.

LEFT: The Old Corner Bookstore was in fact an apothecary shop from its opening in 1718 until 1829. The publishing company that then moved in—Ticknor & Fields—became a meeting place for some of America's most illustrious authors, including Hawthorne, Emerson, and Longfellow, as well as publishing the successful *Atlantic Monthly*.

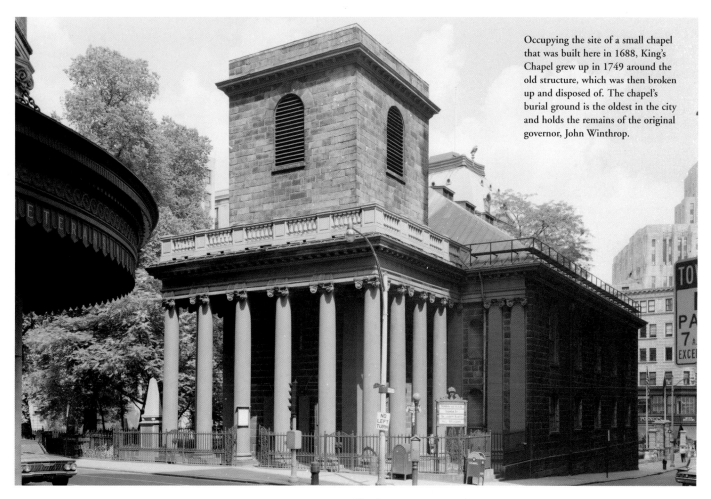

Occupying the site of a small chapel that was built here in 1688, King's Chapel grew up in 1749 around the old structure, which was then broken up and disposed of. The chapel's burial ground is the oldest in the city and holds the remains of the original governor, John Winthrop.

RIGHT: This painting, "View of the Long Wharf and the Harbor of Boston," by J. Byron, dates to 1764 and shows spires rising above a densely built port town. To the left is the steeple of Old North Church, built in 1723.

Revolutionary Boston

As the home of the "Sons of Liberty," led by Samuel Adams, and the site of the Boston Massacre, Boston Tea Party, and some of the earliest and fiercest battles of the American Revolution, Boston was at the heart of the conflict that would change the city, as well as the country, forever. With victory would come a huge surge of growth. Following the war, Boston became one of the largest ports in the world. Attracted by the profits being generated, the population swelled and as wealth spilled into the city's coffers Boston would begin to build grand edifices, as well its reputation as an intellectual center.

Revolutionary fervour had been running high in the city for over ten years before the outbreak of open hostilities. A succession of taxes, imposed to help pay for the recent war against the French were seen as unfair by the colonies, who had no representative at the British parliament, and the flames of indignation were fanned by the killing of five protesters by British troops on March 5, 1770. After the British parliament declared Massachusetts to be in rebellion after the Tea Party of December 16, 1773, the port was closed down on April 1, 1774, and British troops under a new governor, General Thomas Gage, were sent to quell the rebellion. Their arrival heralded the war to come.

Fighting broke out in April 1775 and occupied Boston saw action during the Battles of Lexington, Concord, and Bunker Hill. The city was relieved in March 1776 by General Washington and the British forced to evacuate.

RIGHT: This contemporary drawing of the Boston Massacre shows the moment, on March 5, 1770, when British troops opened fire on the jeering crowd before the Old State House. Five were killed. The tragedy proved a turning point in Boston's, and America's, history. Tensions between the colonists and British, already tense, now reached boiling point and three years after the massacre Bostonians climbed aboard British ships carrying newly taxed tea and turned their cargoes overboard.

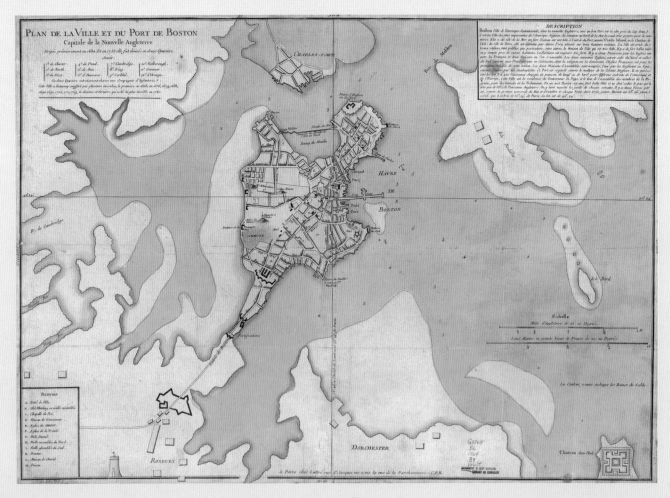

LEFT: This French map of Boston dated to 1775, shows the city on the verge of war. What was a tiny settlement has grown into a bustling town and a center of commerce. Note the length of Long Wharf in the harbor and the fortifications protecting the peninsula on the isthmus connecting it to the mainland.

ABOVE: The fight at Lexington took place on April 19, 1775. This contemporary print shows Minute Men being fired upon by British troops who were sent from Boston to Lexington by Governor Thomas Gage to sieze and destroy the patriots' munitions.

ABOVE: This drawing shows a British fortification on Beacon Hill in the foreground. The key provides details of town features and troop positions. At 9 is "Kops Hill and Battery which played on the Rebels Redout on Bunkers Hill the 17th June." Across the river at 3 is "the Rebels redoubt."

RIGHT: The British were finally forced to flee the city after General Washington occupied Dorchester Heights and threatened to fire cannon down on British troops guarding the city in March 1776. The evacuation marked the first major victory of the United States forces, but was marked by the destruction of Boston Light, which the British blew up as they left.

A view over Boston Harbor from the Charlestown Navy Yard in 1833, showing a city that is starting to grow rapidly behind the ships on which the city's fortunes depended.

The Great Port: 1784–1850

The Great Port: 1784–1850

The creation of the United States signaled a surge in Boston's growth, not only in terms of the city's economy and population, but physically too. As the city rapidly grew into the nation's premier port, with a burgeoning textile industry, the city needed more land and from the beginning of the nineteenth century began to cut down its hills in order to create additional waterfront. Mount Vernon was the first to go, leveled to provide landfill along Charles Street, then between 1807 and 1824, Beacon Hill was used to fill the Mill Pond in the North Cove, joining North End to the rest of Boston. Streets on the new land were laid out by the great Charles Bulfinch. Pemberton Hill was quickly razed in 1835, and filled out the north side of Causeway Street, close by where North Station now stands.

As wealth poured into the city, new grander homes were in demand and Boston began to develop the characteristic Georgian look that distinguishes its historic neighborhoods. Designed or influenced by Charles Bulfinch, whose work on the 1795 plan for the Massachusetts State House was widely admired, mansions were erected on Beacon Hill for and Faneuil Hall was extended, as was Quincy Market and the Charleston Navy Yard. The university city also grew in stature as an intellectual hub, attracting some of the period's greatest writers as well as publishing houses.

While Boston became more gentrified, it simultaneously began to struggle to house the growing tide of immigrants who came to find their fortunes. The city that had numbered barely 25,000 at the beginning of the nineteenth century counted nearly 150,000 citizens by mid-century, many of them Irish refugees fleeing the potato famine of the 1840s.

ABOVE AND RIGHT: The first of Charles Bulfinch's Harrison Gray Otis Houses dates to 1796 and is an excellent example of the architectural style that the architect stamped upon post-revolutionary Boston. Built for a wealthy young entrepreneur and politician, the house is based on the British Georgian style that incorporated Palladian ideals of symmetry. Now serving as a museum, it has been returned to its original condition, including decoration and furnishings that are more boldly colorful than might be expected. Bulfinch went on to design many more buildings of all types around the city and other architects of the time followed where he led.

ABOVE AND RIGHT: Designed by Charles Bulfinch the Massachusetts State House, at the tip of Boston common, opened in 1798 after three years of construction work. (The cornerstone was laid by Samuel Adams and Paul Revere). Beneath a beautiful dome of copper and gold—which would be much copied, not least at the Capitol Building in Washington—the building includes a superb room for the House of Representatives (right), the Nurses Hall, which depicts scenes of the American Revolution, and a main staircase over which are ornate stained glass windows. The wings to either side of the original building were added in 1914.

BELOW AND RIGHT: Dating to the early 1830s, this illustration shows the fort on Castle Island, with Boston in the distance. Now land-bound the island's position made it perfect for defending the city and its first fortifications were built in 1636. Since then eight forts have been built the latest of which is Fort Independence, shown in the black and white photograph. It was dedicated by President John Adams, a Bostonian himself, in 1799.

LEFT: Until it was closed by President Nixon in 1974, Charleston Navy Yard was one of the United States Navy's most important shipyards. It was designed by Alexander Parris (the architect of Quincy Market) and opened in 1800. The decommissioned yard is now a tourist attraction and the berth of the U.S.S. *Constitution*, the oldest ship of the U.S. Navy still afloat.

RIGHT: Built on the edge of the common at Park Street in 1810, Park Street Church is the work of architect Peter Banner, who was influenced by London's Christopher Wren.

EXTERIOR VIEW OF THE BOSTON ATHENÆUM.

LEFT AND RIGHT: The Boston Athenaeum, on Beacon Street, opened in 1807 and combined a large library with a museum of art. The architect of the building was Edward Clarke Cabot, a sheep farmer who based his design on that of the Palazzo da Porta Festa in Vicenza. Its excellent collection contains the library of President George Washington.

ABOVE: Charles Bulfinch's final commission in Boston before he left to oversee the expansion of the United States Capitol in Washington, D.C. was the Bulfinch Pavilion of Massachusetts General Hospital, which was built in 1818. Below the central dome, which floods the area below with light, is a circular operating theater complete with seating for spectators.

RIGHT: Rising above Charlestown, the Bunker Hill Monument is a memorial dedicated to the Battle of Bunker Hill, during which British forces suffered heavy losses at the hands of the victorious patriot army. The cornerstone was laid by Lafayette in 1825, though due to financial difficulties the monument was not actually completed until 1848.

ABOVE AND RIGHT: The Quincy Market buildings were raised in 1826 on the site that had been used as an open-air marketplace since the arrival of the Puritan settlers. Symbolic of Boston's rapid growth at that time, the waterfront area had to be filled in to accommodate the grand building. Originally housing overspill from the Faneuil Hall Market, the building was later named for Mayor Josiah Quincy whose brainchild it was. The black and white image shows the busy marketplace in 1905.

Quincy Market underwent an
extensive restoration in the 1970s and
the 535 foot hall is now a popular
meeting place, filled with restaurants
as well as a nightclub, and, of course,
market stalls.

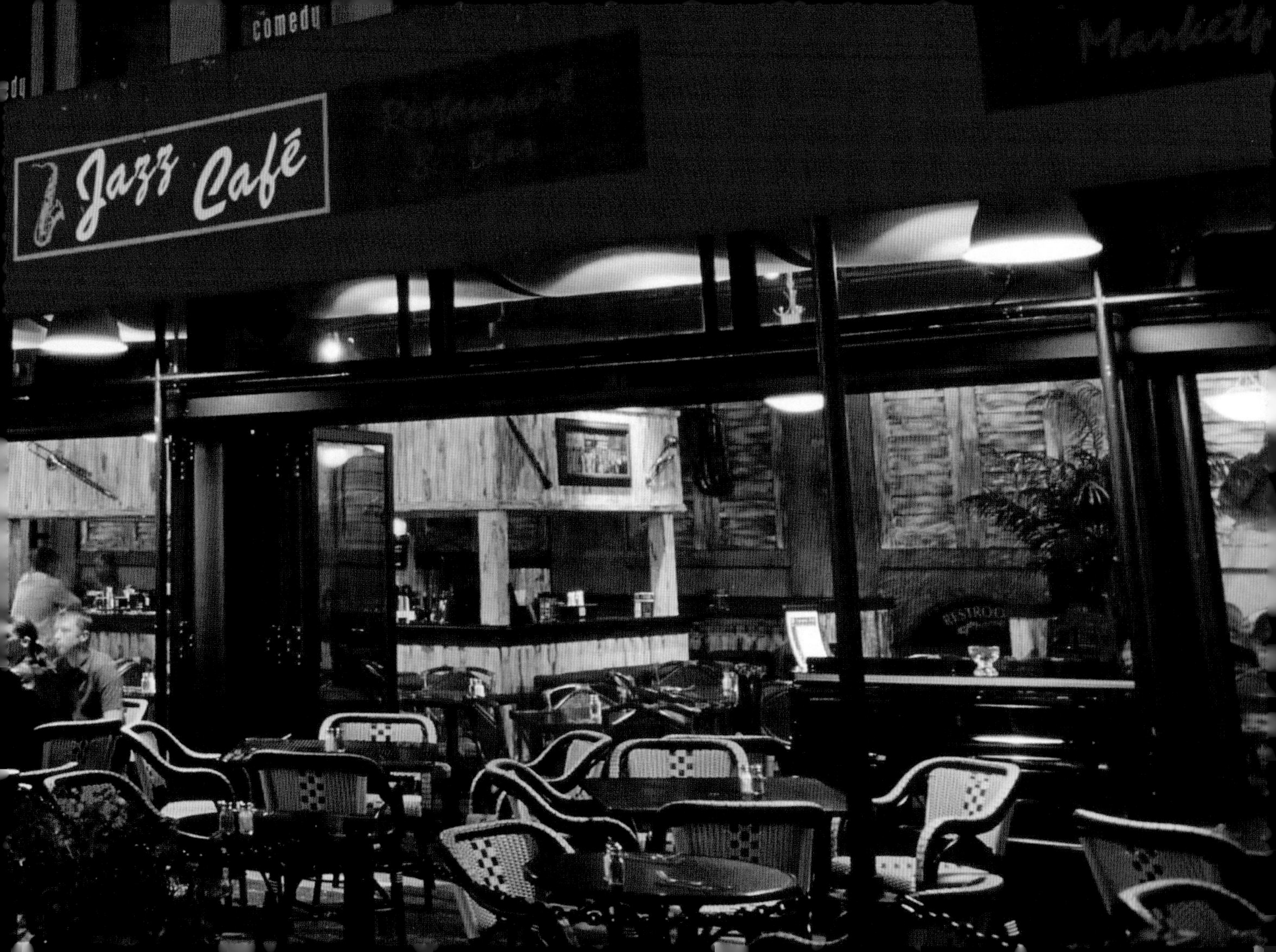
comedy
Jazz Café
RESTROOMS

ABOVE: This undated view of Bowdoin Street on Beacon Hill shows the area in the early to mid-nineteenth century. On the hill is the Beacon Hill Monument, designed by Charles Bulfinch to mark the spot of the Puritans' beacon with a memorial to the revolution. The excavation work is being carried out in order to provide landfill to extend Boston's waterfront.

RIGHT: Beacon Hill's Louisburg Square became the most exclusive address in Boston from the 1830s onward. Over the years the narrow, Palladian-influenced houses that surround the small square have been home to many of the city's most notable families.

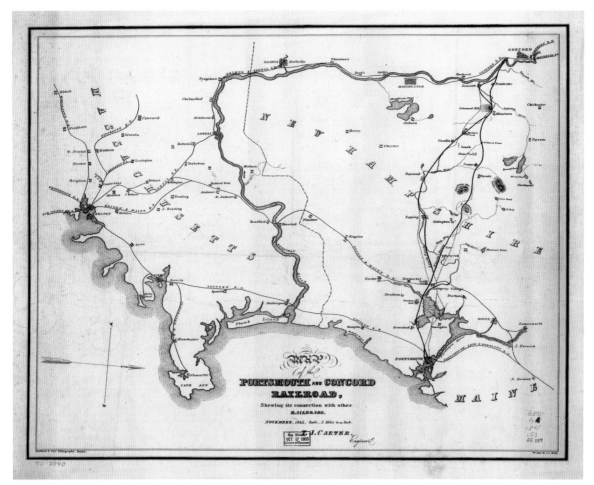

LEFT: From 1835 onward Boston was at the center of an ever expanding network of railway lines that bought goods and raw materials into the city for export via the port or to be worked in Boston's mills and factories. Already a hub of commerce, the railway brought even more wealth to the city. This map shows the tracks of the Portsmouth and Concord Railroad and its connections to other railways about a decade after the first steam train entered the city.

RIGHT: The narrow cobblestoned Acorn Street, on Beacon Hill, was the home of artisans and artists in the early nineteenth century. Today, it is one of the city's most visited—and photographed—sites.

Adjacent to Boston Common the Public Garden is built on land that was reclaimed from swamp in 1839. At its heart is a bronze statue of George Washington that was dedicated in 1869.

ABOVE AND LEFT: Laid out as a formal garden, inspired by French design, Boston Common's English Pond was created in 1861 (the famous swan boats first appeared in 1877).

RIGHT: This painted engraving shows a distant view of Boston in 1841 with ships in the harbor, the "Worcester Rail Road" on the left, the "Lowell Rail Road" on the right, and the Bunker Hill monument in the middle background.

Growth and Destruction: 1851–1900

A view over Back Bay, which was filled in during the second half of the nineteenth century. The second tallest building in the photograph is the Prudential Center, the first skyscraper to be built in the area. Completed in 1964 and measuring 750 feet, it was at that time the tallest building in North America outside of New York City.

Growth and Destruction: 1851–1900

The final decades of the nineteenth century saw the pace of Boston's growth become faster still. In just five decades Boston's population swelled by over 400,000, while the city built museums, parks, universities, and public buildings. From 1857 to 1894 Boston also undertook its most ambitious landfill project yet, creating Back Bay, which would quickly become the city's premier residential district and boast architectural wonders such as Henry Hobson Richardson's Trinity Church. A series of annexations, notably of Roxbury, Dorchester, Brighton, and Charlestown also boosted the size of the city and the number of its citizens while the growth of the railroads saw manufacturing industries eclipsing shipping after the Civil War.

The number of significant buildings and institutions that date to this period are too numerous to mention in full but include, Boston Public Gardens (1859), Boston College (1863), Massachusetts Institute of Technology (1865), Boston University (1869), the Emerald Necklace (1878 onward), the Boston Public Library (1895), and the nation's first subway system (1898). The city also became the first to boast an electrically lit hotel (the Hotel Vendome in 1882) and saw citizens turn out for the first Boston Marathon in 1897.

Punctuating this era of unparalleled expansion was the worst calamity to befall the city in its long history. The Great Boston Fire burned for only twelve hours over November the ninth and tenth, but left a smouldering hole of sixty-five acres in downtown as well as lost fortunes.

Nevertheless, Boston turned the disaster to its advantage, constructing modern industrial buildings that renewed the textile and leatherworking industries. As the nineteenth century ended, the city could look back on an era during which it had more than doubled in size and had become a leading seat of learning and culture.

RIGHT: Occupying a 135-acre campus along the Charles River in Cambridge, the Massachusetts Institute of Technology dates back to 1861 and has developed into one of the world's foremost engineering and science universities. This beautifully hand-colored photograph shows the Rogers Building, the first of many architectural gems to be to be constructed on campus, in 1863.

ABOVE: This tattered photograph shows the aftermath of the Great Boston Fire, which ravaged the city for two days in November 1872. Roughly sixty-five acres of downtown and the Financial District were consumed by flames, at least twenty people died, and tens of millions of dollars worth of damage was caused.

RIGHT: View of the conflagration in Devonshire Street, looking south toward Beebe & Co.'s Buildings, on Winthrop Square. The fire started at about 7.20pm in a dry goods store on Summer Street on November 9, and was not extinguished until the following day.

Back Bay

Beginning in the early nineteenth century a series of landfall projects have added over 3,000 acres to Boston. The first of these saw Mount Vernon, Beacon Hill, and Pemberton Hill cut down to create new land along the waterfront. The most ambitious project, however, was the reclamation of the tidal Back Bay, which lasted from 1857 to 1882. Development on the new land was carefully planned under architect Arthur Gilman and the result was a beautiful neighborhood of brownstone townhouses that was immediately popular with Bostonians. In fact, Back Bay quickly became one of the city's most desirable addresses.

LEFT: With Boston's hills already razed to provide landfill, it was necessary to look further afield for the filling of Back Bay. In fact, most of the gravel used came from Needham to the west, and at the height of the work 3,500 carloads a day were moved from the pits into the city.

RIGHT: At the heart of Back Bay is Commonwealth Avenue, the design of which was inspired by wide Parisian boulevards. This photograph, taken from the leafy central mall, shows the George A. Nickerson House at number 303, one of the grand homes that were built along the avenue.

FOLLOWING PAGE: Today fringed by some of Boston's most notable buildings, including the John Hancock Tower and Trinity Church, Copley Square was a marshy riverbank until 1870.

Trinity Church, designed by Henry Hobson Richardson, is a superb Romanesque edifice of granite and sandstone that was completed in 1877. Inside, the interior design was by John LaFarge, while many of the art glass windows are a result of a collaboration between Edward Burne-Jones and William Morris. During construction, huge foundation plinths were driven through marshy soil to the bedrock beneath.

PREVIOUS PAGE AND RIGHT: While Boston Public Library was originally established in 1848 within a few years its popularity was such that a new, larger, building was needed. The present building on Copley Square was erected between 1887 and 1895 and owes its design to one of America's foremost architects, Charles McKim. Built in an Italianate style the library features exquisite sculptures and murals.

IN HONO
OF THE
SECOND MASSACHUSETTS V

WINCHESTER · 1862 · CEDAR MOUNTAIN ·
ANTIETAM · CHANCELLORSVILLE
GETTYSBURG · RESACA · ATLANTA
THE MARCH TO THE SEA · SAVANNAH

ER INFANTRY
HE

Lined with elegant brownstone rowhouses on wide boulevards, Back Bay is arranged on a strict grid at odds with the twisting streets of older Boston.

LEFT: Boston's first Chinese settlers arrived in the city in the mid-1870s and their numbers swelled as the century drew to a close with workers arriving to take advantage of the jobs available in booming Boston. Centered on Beach Street, the city's Chinatown is now the third largest in the nation.

ABOVE AND OVERLEAF: Washington Street was built in the early nineteenth century to connect the city to the mainland and extended from downtown to Roxbury. As the city's main artery it was soon carrying horse drawn streetcars and, due to the volume of traffic, by the mid-1870s this section (with Downtown Crossing at its heart) was already a busy shopping district. By the turn of the century the streetcars were electric and the area was confirmed as the city's premier shopping destination.

The Emerald Necklace

In 1878 Frederick Law Olmsted was commissioned to create a series of parks that would join Boston Common to Franklin Park in order to provide an escape for inhabitants of the industrial nineteenth century city. Over the next two decades land that was once marsh was landscaped and the Muddy River redirected. The result is the Emerald Necklace, a 1,100 acre chain of open spaces on which are built some of the city's great institutions, such as Museum of Fine Arts, Isabella Stewart Gardner Museum, and Franklin Park Zoo.

RIGHT: An aerial view of the Emerald Necklace, which includes six major parklands as well as community gardens. The layout of the park provides a seven mile walk through parkland from Boston Common to Franklin Park. Although it is not quite possible to walk from one end of the chain to another through continuous parkland, all are very close together.

ABOVE: Visitors to Franklin Park Zoo watch tropical birds in 1914. The small collection of animals has since grown into a world-class zoo in which animals are allowed to live in recreations of their natural habitats.

RIGHT: The second largest of the parks in the necklace's chain, the Arnold Arboretum is a 265 acre area that supports a huge variety of plant species. The collections are maintained and added to by the park's leaseholder, Harvard University.

LEFT: The Fenway link in the Emerald Necklace is home to the Isabella Stewart Gardner Museum, which houses a fine collection of European art including works from the Renaissance as well as Old Masters. A beautifully designed building in the style of an Italian palazzo, this photograph shows the Venetian Courtyard.

ABOVE: Also to be found in the Fenway is the Museum of Fine Arts, which moved to this location in 1909. This photograph shows the European Art collection.

With a collection that encompasses
art and artifacts from ancient times
to contemporary works, the Museum
of Fine Arts is one of America's
foremost art museums.

ABOVE: The Christian Science Center in Boston is the world headquarters for the denomination and occupies fourteen acres of the intersection of Huntington and Massachusetts avenues. The Romanesque Mother Church dates to 1894 while the basilica was completed in 1906. Further offices and libraries were designed by I.M.Pei.

RIGHT: The Tremont Street Subway, or "T" as it is known locally, was America's first subway system and opened its service between Park Street and Boylston Street on September 1, 1897.

This series of four panoramic photographs were taken from the top of Ames Tower in 1897 and show Boston to the north (left), south (below), east (right), and west (below right). In the years since the end of the American Revolution Boston has become a major center of commerce and industry with a population that has grown from under 20,000 in 1790 to over 560,000.

Modern Boston: 1901–Today

Costing almost $300 million, the
Stata Center on the campus of the
Massachusetts Institute of
Technology was designed by the
Internationally renowned Frank
Gehry and opened in 2004.

Modern Boston: 1901–Today

Like so many cities around the world, the twentieth century brought troubled times to Boston. Prosperity lasted through the early years and the city continued to build, notably the Museum of Fine Arts in 1909 and Fenway Park in 1912, but the great rush of building projects slowed and then ground to a halt in the twenties and thirties. The city's economy, which had become so dependent on manufacturing during the Industrial Revolution, began to decline as industry moved southward where labor was cheaper.

Hastened by the Great Depression of the thirties, by the 1950s Boston was experiencing a full-blown slump. With a population at an all-time high of over 800,000 this was a disaster for the city and left thousands unemployed. Once seen as the heart of intellectual America, city officials also took the city back to its Puritan roots, banning books, movies, and plays that contained any hint of immorality. The city's prospects were hardly brightened by the wanton destruction of neighborhoods such the West End and

VIEW OF BOSTON HARBOR - FR

Scollay Square to make way for the Central Artery and government buildings. The "urban renewal" cost thousands of families their homes, closed businesses, and saw historic buildings lost forever.

Nevertheless, Boston began to revive in the 1960s and over the following years it would leave its industrial past behind and become a center of finance, medicine, and high-tech business. Renewal that had been so careless was now carried out more sensitively in the face of local pressure and a booming tourist industry. The city's skyline also began to rise with the construction of skyscrapers in Back Bay such as Prudential Tower (1965) and the John Hancock Tower (1976). As the twentieth century drew to a close, Boston began to reverse the vandalism of previous years,

beginning the "Big Dig" that would widen the congested Central Artery and place it underground.

Now a thoroughly modern city yet boasting charming winding Colonial streets, beautifully preserved architecture, and a sense of its own heritage, Boston remains one of America's most delightful cities.

A panoramic view over Boston Harbor in 1912 shows the waterfront crowded with wharves, warehouses, and tenement buildings that would have housed Boston's immigrant population. At this time the city's population would have been overwhelmingly made up of Irish who had been flooding into the city since the middle of the previous century.

F OF N.E. TEL. & TEL. CO'S B'LD'G. -

LEFT: Boston over the buildings of the Beach & Clarridge Co. factory in 1902 with smoke pouring from the chimneys of various factories and mills. While New York had taken over from Boston as the United States' busiest port with the opening of the Erie Canal in 1825, Boston remained a manufacturing and commercial hub with textile manufacturing and leatherwork among its most significant industries.

ABOVE: This 1903 view of Boylston Street and Tremont Street shows the Colonial Theater (far left), which opened at the end of 1900 as well as the Hotel Touraine (center, with the curved corner), with the Masonic Temple opposite.

ABOVE: The junction of
Commonwealth Avenue and Beacon
Street in Back Bay in 1903.

This aerial view of the city from 1905 shows the extent to which landfill and annexations have increased the size of Boston by the beginning of the twentieth century. Former satellites that had been annexed in the previous century included Washington Village, part of South Boston (1855), Roxbury (1868), West Roxbury (1874), Brighton (1874), and Charleston (1874).

Two photographs that illustrate the changes in Boston's waterfront. The black and white photograph shows the docks in 1910 when it was a maze of vast warehouses and wharves built to accommodate the ever-bigger steam ships that plied the harbor. At this time the city was at the peak of its industrial success. Today, the waterfront has been redeveloped into upscale apartments and office buildings, such as the distinctive circular 2 International Place, which was completed in 1992.

BELOW AND RIGHT: Seen here under construction for the first World Series in 1912, the first ballgame at Fenway Park took place on April 20 of that year, with the Boston Red Sox playing against the New York Highlanders (the Red Sox won 7-6). One of America's best loved ballparks, Fenway Park has changed little over the past ten decades.

FENWAY PARK

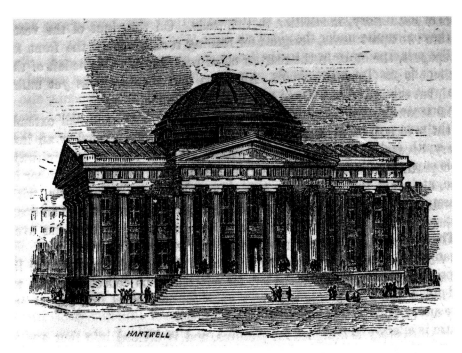

HARTWELL

Once standing at the water's edge, before landfill moved the shoreline away, Custom House was originally built as a domed edifice in 1847. In 1915 however, the dome was removed and replaced with the distinctive 495 foot tower that for many years was the tallest structure in the city.

LEFT: Despite Boston's commercial and industrial might and wealth, for many life was hard. Immigrants pouring into the city were forced to live in tenements or slums such as this one along the waterfront.

RIGHT: Now known as the Opera House, the highly ornate theater on Washington Street was originally named the B.F. Keith Memorial Theater. It opened in 1928 as a stage for vaudeville productions and later was used as a movie theater before the Opera Company of Boston moved in during 1950. The new millennium has seen the building receive an extensive facelift and it now stages Broadway hit musicals.

Boston's Museum of Science was built on a dam
across the Charles River in 1951 and has since grown
out into the Science Park.

The mid-fifties saw the destruction of many old granite and brick buildings in Boston's downtown and their replacement with modern structures such as Government Center Plaza (seen here), John F. Kennedy Towers, Center Plaza, and the new Boston City Hall. Widely criticized, the destruction of fifty-six acres of historic district led preservationists to ensure that the same would never happen again.

John F. Kennedy Federal Building was built at Cambridge Street between 1964 and 1966. The twenty-four storey building is connected to a five storey structure by a glass-enclosed walkway, and features an exposed atrium between and two buildings as well as a two story lobby area.

Seen here just after its completion in 1968, Boston's futuristic New City Hall, at City Hall Plaza, owes its design to the architectural firm of Kallmann, McKinnell & Knowles. Housing offices for the municipal government, it also has spaces for music performances and art exhibitions.

BELOW AND FOLLOWING PAGE:
Completed in 1969, the New
England Aquarium on Central Wharf
has become one of the waterfront's
most popular attractions.
Incorporated into the design of the
building is a huge tank that recreates
ocean conditions and is home to a
variety of sealife.

ABOVE: Created in 1976 as part of a project to renew and restore Boston's waterfront, Christopher Columbus Park is surrounded by wisteria and offers wonderful views over the water.

Seen here at dusk, John Hancock Tower is the city's tallest building, and the highest in New England. Rising 790 feet, it was designed by I.M. Pei and completed in 1976. The exterior is sheathed with 10,344 panes of reflective glass.

Overlooking Boston Harbor from Columbia Point in Dorchester, the John F. Kennedy Library and Museum was designed by I. M. Pei and built in 1979.

Rowe's Wharf was designed by the internationally renowned architectural firm of Skidmore, Owings & Merrill and was completed in 1987. Including a luxury hotel, marina, condos, and office space, the development is the epitome of the new waterfront.

Post Office Square is a calm and leafy park in the center of the Financial District that was built on the site of a garage that was demolished in 1990. The photograph shows the fountain made of green glass on the Pearl Street side of the square.

LEFT: Completed in 2006 after decades of planning and construction, the "Big Dig" moved the six-lane Central Artery through downtown underground and, at nearly fifteen billion dollars, was the most expensive engineering project in U.S. history. The completion of the project saw areas once occupied by noisy and polluted raised concrete highways transformed into green space.

Built as part of the Big Dig, Leonard P. Zakim Bunker Hill Bridge was the widest cable-stayed bridge in the world when it opened in 2003. Crossing the Charles River, the bridge is the northen entrance to, and exit from, the city.

Photo credits

PREVIOUS PAGE: Boston is a city of dramatic contrasts. While no longer one of the nation's largest cities, what it lacks in size it more than makes up for in stature.